ABIGAIL THO

Scribbly Gum Nature Diary

Year-round adventures with Australia's plants and animals

ABC Books

Published by ABC Books for the
AUSTRALIAN BROADCASTING CORPORATION
GPO Box 9994 Sydney NSW 2001

First published in 2006

National Library of Australia
Cataloguing-in-Publication entry
Thomas, Abigail.
Scribbly gum nature diary : year-round adventures with Australia's plants and animals.

Includes index.
For children aged 8 – 12.
ISBN 0 7333 1583 6.
1. Natural history – Australia – Juvenile literature.
I. Australian Broadcasting Corporation. II. Title.
508.94

Cover and internal design by Melanie Young, Inhouse Graphic Design
Front cover photographs courtesy of Jason Dare, Stephen Lin, Keith Power, Nick Vane, Peter Chew, Sean Phillipson and the Australian Koala Foundation
Back cover photographs courtesy of Alf Adams, Lyn Lowe, Sean Phillipson and Greg Brown
Colour reproduction by Graphic Print Group, Adelaide
Printed by SNP Leefung Printers Ltd, China

5 4 3 2 1

What's happening when

January

Crocodiles seek mates in the steamy swamps up north, while cicadas call and scribbly gum trees shed their bark. Off the coast, Pygmy Blue Whales enjoy a rare feast.

February

Dragonflies hunt prey, as orb spiders begin to spin their enormous webs, and baby blue-tongues appear in the garden. Fairy Penguins shed last year's feathers.

March

Myna birds cause trouble, as mistletoe bursts into flower. Thunderstorm clouds pile up and bring the rain that turns frogs' eggs into tadpoles and tadpoles into frogs.

What's happening when

April

Powerful owls give more than two hoots, while turtles go walkabout and Tassie Devils scream for a mate. King Tides invade Australia's northern beaches and towns.

May

Mountain Pygmy-possums snooze beneath snow, while native bees nap in nests. But some gum trees still bloom brilliantly and the tiny silvereye bird flies north for winter.

June

Brolga birds dance an ancient jig, while echidnas form a conga line of love. Ants tenderly look after butterflies and the corroboree frog chills out in frozen ponds.

What's happening when

July

Lonely platypus cruise the rivers, while heavy winter wattles bloom overhead. Hungry potoroos dig up stinking native truffles and crow butterflies snuggle up to stay safe.

August

Magpies dive-bomb terrified postmen, as emu chicks start to hatch out. Dugongs swim to warmer waters and daredevil pilots head north to surf the Morning Glory.

September

West Australian wildflowers light up the landscape, while ladybirds go on a killing spree. Animals leave behind telltale scats and humpbacks migrate north.

What's happening when

October

Koalas bellow out for a mate, while cockatoos go on an urban rampage. Malleefowls build gigantic desert nests and tropical corals pour a cloud of pink into the water.

November

Blue-ringed octopus hatch out and baby quolls quit the pouch. Bogong moths fly south to cool caves, while gaudy grasshoppers put their colours on for summer.

December

Beetles are out and easy to find, while pythons hunt for plump rats and cassowary dads fuss over their chicks. Dangerous lightning storms burn power poles around Darwin.

Introduction

The first willy wagtail of spring, the peeling bark of the apple gum to reveal a brilliant pink trunk, the growling of crocodiles on heat and the dazzling display of wildflowers in Western Australia — all these events shout out that the season is changing. As days lengthen, temperatures rise and rainfall increases, the Australian bush and its wildlife respond in some truly amazing ways.

Australia is an enormous island which stretches 4,000 kilometres from east to west. Yet despite all this space, 90 per cent of our population is squeezed into towns and cities. Living in an urban environment, where the house next door blocks the morning sun or the heat rising from the footpath dissolves the cool evening breezes, it's easy to forget that above, below and all around us, the cycles of nature go on, just as they always have.

For instance, hundreds of birds still pass through our towns and cities on their yearly migration, although we may not hear their songs above the traffic. But if we remember to listen, we can hear many of them calling, just as they do in the bush, to find new mates, claim territory and keep tabs on their young.

In the same way, insects, spiders and other invertebrates can be found in parks and gardens, building their nests and webs but perhaps using a clothes line as an anchor point, rather than the branch of a tree.

Although we have altered our own lives by building cities, creating roads and mass transit systems, and relying on artificial light to determine our

Introduction

own daily activities, we are really just a thin layer of existence balancing on a much deeper and far more ancient system. The seasons as they change — the days getting shorter then longer, the rainfall increasing and then dwindling with the months — are still there, influencing everything around us.

With these seasonal changes come a whole host of responses by Australia's wild animals and plants: the warming of the ground as summer approaches and the first rains trigger many insects to crawl out from their burrows in the soil, take flight and look for a mate. The rising floodwaters in the northern wet season urge crocodiles to begin their summer courtship; the ocean currents off the coast of Western Australia provide a banquet of krill for migrating Pygmy Blue Whales; the cooling, foggy days of approaching winter cause fungi spore, lying dormant in the soil, to burst forth into a bizarre gallery of brightly coloured and weirdly shaped mushrooms, toadstools and truffles.

Indigenous Australians have known all about these seasonal cycles and lived by their rules for thousands of years. Once you know what to look out for, you realise nature carries on with its yearly rituals, regardless of where we live or how we live our own lives. I hope this book will be enjoyed by all those who love the Australian bush and go some way towards helping to rediscover and enjoy the amazing changes in nature that the seasons bring about.

Scribbly gum tree moulting

Field Notes:

The trunk of a scribbly gum is a smooth whitish yellow and the tree can grow up to 10 metres.

WHEN: Scribbly gum trees moult over summer and produce creamy flowers during winter and spring.

WHERE: Scribbly gums of various species are found across eastern and south-eastern Australia.

WHAT TO LOOK OUT FOR: crazy squiggly lines covering the tree trunk indicate a grub is busy in there.

© Neil Saunders

You could mistake these squiggly marks for graffiti but they are actually made by a hungry, burrowing grub.

The Scribbly gum tree is a lovely eucalyptus tree, with a trunk that looks like someone has scrawled ancient and mysterious writing all over it. These startling patterns are an iconic sight in the Australian bush, and inspired the illustrations in May Gibbs' famous children's book, *Snugglepot and Cuddlepie*. The 'scribbles' are actually made by the grub of a tiny moth *Ogmograptis scribula*. As the grub burrows between the layers of bark, feeding on the sap of the tree, it leaves behind tunnels. These come to an abrupt halt wherever a grub stops burrowing and starts to pupate. The bark of the tree is deciduous, and when the tree moults during summer and the old bark falls away these tunnels are revealed as the scribbles.

While the trees show the evidence of the moth's hard work, the insect itself is rarely seen. The moths are grey and very small (one to two millimetres). Despite covering the trunk with its hieroglyphics, the moth and its larvae are harmless to the tree. Although the moth lives on many different eucalypts, only a few species such as *E.haemostoma*, *E.racemosa* or *E.sclerophylla* display the distinctive scribbly pattern. The moth lays its eggs mostly on *E.rossii* around Canberra and on *E.haemostoma* around Sydney, and in these areas the scribbles are a good character for identifying the tree. However in other parts of Australia the scribbles appear on different eucalypt species.

The thickness of the scribbles increases as the grub grows, until eventually the line stops, showing where the grub has started to pupate.

Pygmy Blue Whales Feasting

It's summer, and Pygmy Blue Whales are swimming down from Indonesia and gathering at two very special places off the coast of Australia. One is a deep ocean canyon called the Rottnest Trench, several hours boat ride from Perth. The other is an area of ocean just off Portland, Victoria.

Whales are attracted to these areas because of the great seafood banquet they can find there — masses of krill (tiny prawn-like creatures) accumulate in these areas to feed off the rich nutrients rising from the deep water below. The whales sieve the bright red, centimetre-long creatures using huge fringed baleen plates hanging from their upper jaw.

Despite their name, Pygmy Blue Whales are actually quite enormous — the females grow up to 22 metres long. But they are puny by comparison with true blue whales, which reach up to 30 metres long. Like blue whales, Pygmies make deep, spooky calls to other whales hundreds of kilometres away. First there's a very long multi-toned 'groan' that lasts about two minutes. This sing is repeated for up to six hours.

We are lucky to have the few hundred Pygmy Blues left that we do – they were massively fished out along with other whale species in the first half of the twentieth century. On one whaling trip alone, a single Russian factory ship took 296 whales of this species. Today they are safe from fishing and blue whale numbers may be growing as fast as seven per cent each year. But they will only be with us as long as there is international agreement that the species should be protected.

Field Notes:

Pygmy Blue Whales are actually pale mottled grey in colour. But seen in the clear oceanic waters, they take on an intense blue colour, giving them their name.

WHEN: Western Australia: February to April; Victoria: December to May

WHERE: off the coast of south-west WA and south-west Victoria.

WHAT TO LOOK OUT FOR: A Pygmy Blue Whale can be distinguished from other whales by its tiny dorsal fin located near the tail. The fin appears as it breaks the surface to breathe.

© Peter Gill, Blue Whale Study

Researchers are tracking the migration of Pygmy Blue Whales by shooting satellite trackers into their blubber.

Crocodiles mating

Field Notes:

Crocodiles were once shot indiscriminately and they became so rare that they were declared a protected species in 1971. But since then, their numbers have built up again from 3,000 to about 60,000, and one day it may be made legal again to hunt crocodiles for sport.

WHERE: Northern Territory, far north Queensland

WHEN: October through to January

WHAT TO LOOK OUT FOR: Two-metre-high nest of mud and sticks; mud tracks on river banks where crocs haul out.

© Brett Crich

Hungry young crocs wait to be fed: one medium-sized wild pig will keep them going for weeks.

As the first rains of the wet season fall, crocodiles in Australia's tropical north start looking for love. During courtship crocs let out deep growls and swim together for hours up and down the billabongs. To establish a new relationship, male crocs will swim underneath the female and blow bubbles up at her, which fizz pleasantly on her soft underbelly, just like a spa bath.

Crocs build a huge nest of branches and leaves glued together with mud. Inside, up to 60 eggs are laid and the warm sun incubates them for 10 weeks. If you listen closely to a nest, you might hear the squawks of the newly hatched babies inside. These calls tell the mother it's time to help dig her babies out of the nest. She carries them carefully down to the river and then stays with them for about a month until they learn to hunt and to fend for themselves.

Although crocs are very fierce, they are also very vulnerable while they are growing up. Only about 10 in every thousand eggs laid will survive through to adulthood. Along the way are many dangers, including flooded nests, raiding pigs and water bird predators. Crocodiles are also cannibalistic, so young crocs face the regular risk of being eaten by their neighbour!

The main purpose of a croc's 'death roll' is to help them tear pieces of flesh off their prey, because crocodiles can't chew up their food. Also, their stomachs are only about the size of a basketball, so food needs to be eaten in quite small chunks. One meal of a turtle or wild pig can keep a croc going for weeks or even months.

Cicadas singing

Summer wouldn't be the same without the deafening call of cicadas filling the warm days. And collecting their brown shells, left discarded on tree trunks, is a must for any treasure hunter who wants to start a natural history collection. Cicadas are officially the world's loudest insects — their calls can reach up to 120dB, or about the same level of noise as a canon going off! No wonder their calls act as a protective mechanism to help to keep hungry birds away.

Although there are over 220 species of cicada around Australia, the best known are the Black Prince, Green Grocer, Double Drummer, Cherrynose, Floury Baker, Redeye, Yellow Monday, Bladder Cicada and Hairy Cicada.

The noisy cicadas we hear are the adults, which live from a few days up to a couple of months. After mating they lay their eggs in slits in tree branches. These hatch into nymphs, which fall to the ground and then dig down into the soil. Here they stay for anything from nine months to 17 years, eventually emerging to crawl up a tree, moult and fly away.

People in countries such as Papua New Guinea eat cicadas, where they are sometimes roasted and taste a bit like chicken. Cicadas are also believed by some to have healing properties. The wings have been used in Chinese medicine, and the bodies used as a diuretic in France, and as a cure for earache in China and Japan. The ancient Greeks believed cicadas symbolised immortality, because they were seen to emerge from the earth, as if they had died and come back to life.

Field Notes:

Cicadas are difficult to keep alive in captivity. They'll only stay alive for a day or two, because they must feed off the flowing sap from a living tree. If you want to keep one alive, cut a big branch and make sure the cut end is in water, but it needs to be replaced every second day. It's probably best to enjoy your cicada for a few hours then let it go.

WHERE: Australia wide

WHEN: December, January

WHAT TO LOOK OUT FOR: brown insect cases on tree trunks

With its body like a bag full of air, the Bladder Cicada makes a low purring call at dusk.

Dragonflies appear

Field Notes:

Dragonflies live in many habitats, from waterfalls in rainforests to high snowy mountains.

WHERE: Dragonflies can be seen all over Australia, but Giant Dragonflies are found only in small pockets.

WHEN: Adult dragonflies emerge from October to November through until late January.

WHAT TO LOOK OUT FOR: Dragonfly wings stick out sideways, whereas damselfly wings fold backwards.

Dragonflies look delicate but they are formidable predators around the creek as they catch their prey on the wing.

One of the loveliest insects to be seen during summer once buzzed around the heads of dinosaurs. Dragonflies existed for millions of years, long before mammals first appeared. One of the most amazing is the Giant Dragonfly, with a wingspan as wide as the length of a large banana.

There are at least four species of Giant Dragonflies native to Australia. These mega-dragonflies are found in south-east Australia, Perth and in the rainforests of Queensland. During February, they are busy flying around and laying their eggs in a peat bog, a kind of soggy pond filled with thick spongy moss. This rare habitat was once mined for garden material, but is now protected to ensure the dragonfly's survival.

Some dragonfly species spend most of their life — perhaps up to several years — living underwater. The larvae looks nothing at all like the flying adult, with an appearance more like an earwig or a silverfish than a flying insect. The larvae are amazing eaters and will devour worms much larger than themselves.

Adult dragonflies are lethal killers too. They catch their prey by forming a basket with their spiny front and middle legs, then hovering over a potential snack, surveying it with their five eyes and manoeuvring backwards and forwards until they are in exactly the right spot to close in for the kill. As the early summer sun warms the water, the larvae crawls out onto a rock and splits its skin. As its new wings expand and dry out, it transforms into an iridescent flying beauty, virtually unchanged from its ancestors, hundreds of millions of years ago.

Blue-tongue babies

In January and February, baby blue-tongue lizards are born all across Australia. Unlike many other reptiles, blue-tongues have live babies, not eggs. The mother gives birth to up to 21 young, and within a month they are gobbling up slugs, snails and spiders, making them a real bonus in the garden. Watch out though, they also like to steal the dog's food! When fully grown, blue-tongues can reach a whopping 60 centimetres long.

Blue-tongues are not actually lizards at all, but members of the skink family. There are seven different species of blue-tongue found around Australia, including the Orange Blotched Blue-Tongue and the Eastern Blue-Tongue.

Sometimes when you walk up to a blue-tongue or find one on the road, it will rear back and try to scare you by opening its mouth wide to show its brilliant blue tongue and bright pink mouth. But it's mostly bluff — the bite of the blue-tongue is not venomous, and if you do get bitten, their peg-like teeth won't usually break the skin. But think twice before picking one up, as their strong jaws can grip hard and leave a bruise!

Scientists have put radio transmitters on blue-tongues and have found that they like to move incredibly long distances. One adult male was found to have crossed 15 backyards and several roads in a single day during his search for a mate.

Blue-tongues make great pets. They live up to 20 years in nothing more than an old fish tank fitted with a 100-watt bulb for warmth. They feed on raw or cooked meat, insects, snails, fruit and bran mash.

Field Notes:

If you want to encourage blue-tongues to your garden, leave short sections of hollow pipe lying around. These make an excellent refuge for the reptiles and give them somewhere to escape to if they are being attacked. Dogs and cats kill blue-tongues, especially younger animals.

WHERE: Australia wide

WHEN: January and February

WHAT TO LOOK OUT FOR:

Lizards often sun themselves by the back door or near the clothes line.

© Jason Dare

Unlike many lizards, blue-tongues have live babies, rather than eggs. This is the best time of year to see them.

orb spiders spinning

Field Notes:

Spiders often build their web in annoying places, like across doorways. Gently remove the web, allowing the spider a chance to get away without becoming entangled. Take the spider to another part of the garden. Spiders rarely rebuild their web in a place where it has been removed more than once or twice.

WHERE: Australia wide

WHEN: January and February

WHAT TO LOOK OUT FOR:
Large wheel-shaped web

© Alf Adams

Not so Incey Wincey, orb-weaving spiders can grow to an enormous size and weave webs strong enough to catch birds.

It's late at night and you're walking up your front path. Suddenly you feel a sticky thread wrap itself around your face — you grab it and the stuff sticks to your hands. Now it's in your hair, but where is the occupant!?

Chances are it's an orb weaver, a group of spiders distinguished by the circular web they spin. There are hundreds of species of orb spider across Australia. Some of the best known are the St Andrews Cross Spider, the hairy Garden Spider and the huge Golden Orb Weaver.

The orb weaver's craft represents the supreme achievement of the spider world. More primitive spiders like trap-doors and funnel webs run after their prey while using their webs mostly for shelter and protecting eggs. But orbs go for a more high-tech approach: they just spin their web, and wait.

Orbs can spin several types of web — one sticky, the other smooth. The smooth web is spun into a framework like the spokes of a wheel, which enables the spider to move about without being caught in its own web. Then the sticky web is woven into a spiral on top of the framework.

At this time of year, orbs are fat from months of feeding and ready to mate. When he has found a female, the male attracts her attention by gently tapping on her web. In some species, the female is 20 times larger than the male — and she often tries to eat him after they have mated. To fool her, he may even leave one of his legs behind in her web as a decoy!

Fairy Penguins moulting

It's sunset and just off a beach in Victoria the water ripples and swirls. Suddenly, dozens of small penguins burst out of the surf and go waddling furiously up the beach, calling 'Huck! Huck! Huck!' The birds are returning from their daily fishing trip to the shelter of their burrows on land. Measuring a compact 30 centimetres, Fairy (also called Little, or Blue) Penguins weigh only about a kilogram. The back of their bodies is bluish-grey, the front is white and their wings are black.

Fairy Penguins are still to be found along the coast from Perth, Western Australia to Coffs Harbour, New South Wales. Once common along the beaches, Fairy Penguins are now mainly restricted to offshore islands, given the continual pressure on survival from cars, roads and dogs. But it's still possible to see them, particularly on Phillip Island in Victoria and Kangaroo Island in South Australia, where large permanent colonies exist. There's even a small colony living in busy Sydney Harbour, where they delight the local yachties as they paddle around and fish for their supper.

At this time of the year, penguins are feeding up big before the breeding season. They spend up to three weeks at sea gorging themselves on fish and then return to land to moult. Then they are ready for breeding, and often start by seeking out last year's nesting burrow. After a quick spring clean, it's as good as new. Many also seek out last year's partner, and one penguin 'couple' near Perth are known to have paired up every breeding season for the past 12 years!

Field Notes:

Penguins don't sleep at night, but have frequent micro-sleeps of a few minutes duration to keep them fresh.

WHERE: New South Wales, Victoria, South Australia, Western Australia, Tasmania

WHEN: In New South Wales, Victoria and Tasmania, penguins are feeding up before they moult.

WHAT To Look OUT FoR: Penguins float on the surface to rest in between diving for fish. They fish at sea during the day and come ashore at night.

© Phillip Island Nature Parks

Penguins on parade: this nightly ritual on Phillip Island is enjoyed by millions of visitors every year.

Misunderstood mistletoe

Field Notes:

The seed of the mistletoe is spread by the Mistletoe bird, a brilliant red, black-and-white bird the size of a sparrow.

WHERE: Australia wide

WHEN: Flowers and fruits all year round, depending on the species.

WHAT TO LOOK OUT FOR: one of the easiest to spot is the Drooping Mistletoe, which attaches itself to old roadside eucalyptus trees throughout the eastern states.

© Lui Weber

Slippery little suckers: mistletoes thrive off the sap of other plants but are beneficial for wildlife.

Just like ticks and worms, some plants are parasitic too — stealing their food from the living tissues of other plants. The best-known plant parasites are the mistletoe plants, which begin life as a tiny sticky seed, ejected from the bottom of a bird that has eaten the mistletoe fruit. This sticky seed if deposited on a branch of the right kind of tree will sprout and begin growing. They particularly like eucalypts, acacias and casuarinas.

The seed quickly grows a special root which burrows right through the tree bark and finds its way in, where it starts to share in the tree's own sap. A single mature gum tree can have up to 20 mistletoe plants growing on it and stealing a substantial portion of the host tree's water and minerals.

About 90 species of mistletoe are found only in Australia, and many mimick their hosts. They look so much like the leaves of the host tree that it's sometimes hard to tell if there is mistletoe there at all. One of the most spectacular mistletoes is the West Australian Christmas tree, the largest mistletoe in the world. It seeks out the roots of other trees in the same way airborne mistletoe grows on branches. In their search for food, the clasping roots have been known to invade water pipes and even plastic-wrapped telephone cables!

But mistletoes aren't as bad as they seem. Their nectar-laden flowers, which for many species bloom during autumn, are much prized by native birds and animals. The bushy shape of mistletoe also provides a great place for possums and birds to build their nests.

Severe storms

The blinding rains and gusty winds of severe storms can strike at any time, from summer to winter. While the storm season for eastern Australia is coming to a close at this time of the year, the northern Australian storms are just cranking up. But what is, officially, a severe storm? The Bureau of Meteorology says there has to be very big hail stones (larger than two centimetres), flash flooding, or winds blowing at more than 90 kph (strong enough to tear off a roof).

Severe storms are born in thunderclouds, those massive piled-up clouds, 15 kilometres high that look like a marshmallow castle. Warm humid air rises and combines with the cold air above, causing instability in the atmosphere and generating strong updrafts. These updrafts can only hold moisture in the air for so long before it comes pouring down as rain. This is the type of rain that causes flash flooding, and as much as 200 millimetres can fall in a single hour. If conditions are cold enough, hail is also formed. This happens when small particles of ice circulate within storm clouds, accumulating more icy layers. Cut a hail stone in half and you'll see it's made up of concentric layers of ice.

Predicting storms is a tricky business, but they usually happen in the afternoon, when the sunbaked ground heats the air above and forces it to rise. Despite all the technology, the Bureau of Meteorology can only predict how severe a storm will be about an hour ahead, so if there's a huge black cloud outside and it's looking nasty, it's best to stay indoors!

Field Notes:

Storm chasers are people who deliberately follow storms, photograph them and record how they behave.

WHEN: autumn (northern Australia); spring/summer (eastern Australia); winter (South Australia)

WHERE: Australia wide, particularly in the north.

WHAT TO LOOK OUT FOR: Look for darkish green or grey clouds accumulating late in the afternoon of a warm day.

© Skot Biner

A spectacular thunderhead cloud brews up a mighty lightning storm to relieve the tension of a hot summer afternoon.

Myna birds invade

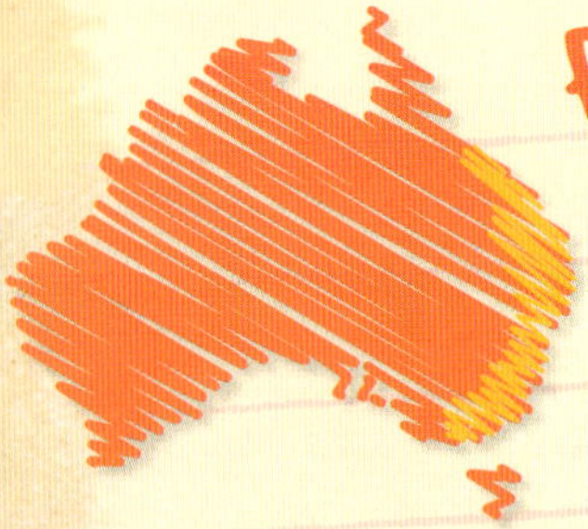

Field Notes:

Mynas nest in the roofs of houses and can spread mites and asthma to human inhabitants.

WHERE: East and south-east inland Australia, at least as far as Albury.

WHEN: form large flocks in autumn, but obvious all year round.

WHAT TO LOOK OUT FOR: A brown-and-black bird with a yellow eye patch and a raucous call. They often strut about on the ground and love roosting in palm trees.

Aptly named the flying cane toad, Indian Mynas are probably the most unpopular birds in Australia.

The Common or Indian Myna bird is fast becoming Australia's number one feral enemy, earning it the dubious title of 'Flying Cane Toad'. During autumn, Indian Mynas are especially noticeable as they start to form large flocks. In just a few decades, this cocky brown-and-black bird with the yellow eye patch has spread from a few isolated spots to invade many eastern and southern cities and towns.

From a few individual birds brought in to Australia in the 1800s to control insects in Melbourne's market gardens, the Indian Myna now poses one of the biggest threats to Australia's native bird life. It's worrying because it competes aggressively with native birds for nest sites and food. The highly intelligent myna bird will even go to the trouble of filling up nearby vacant tree hollows with rubbish to prevent other birds from using them as nests.

The myna eats almost anything and especially loves overflowing garbage bins and rubbish dumps. As more becomes known about Indian Myna behaviour and biology, many communities are taking action to rid their areas of the birds. To discourage foraging, some petrol stations and fast food outlets are covering over their garbage bins. Several councils have stopped the planting of exotic palm trees around shopping centres because mynas love to nest in them. A trap has even been designed especially to catch myna birds and no others, and is now being used to remove the birds from infested areas.

Tadpoles on the hop

The change from tadpole into frog is one of the most amazing things to see in nature. At this time of the year, the autumn rains inspire many frogs to lay one more batch of tadpole eggs. But once they hatch, tadpoles aren't as easy to find as you might think. Most hide from predators in the mud at the bottom of a pond or creek, only rising to the surface for air.

Tadpoles take between six weeks and three months to turn into frogs, depending on the species. Some desert frogs change in just 16 days, while the barred frog takes two years to turn from tadpole into frog! Metamorphosis is often brought on by rising temperatures or food shortages.

Over 200 species of frog have been discovered in Australia. One of the strangest is the Western Australian Turtle Frog, which looks like a baby turtle without a shell. It spends much of its life underground in sandy soils and feeds on termites. The South Australian Water Holding Frog also lives mainly underground, enclosed in a cocoon made from layers of shed skin. It stores huge amounts of water in its bladder and the pockets of its skin.

Although some frogs, such as the green tree frog, are flourishing in human environments, many species have suffered dramatic population declines since the 1980s. This may be due to an introduced fungus and to climate change. Fifteen species of frogs are currently endangered, 12 are listed as vulnerable and four have become extinct.

Field Notes:

It is legal to keep some species of tadpoles at home, as long as they are released after they turn into frogs. They eat boiled lettuce or spinach and need clean water.

WHERE: Australia wide

WHEN: Frogs breed all year round but mainly during spring and summer.

WHAT TO LOOK OUT FOR: Use a torch to hunt for frogs calling at night around dams and creeks. Their eyes will glow if you point the light their way.

© Euan Ritchie

Green tree frogs are usually a welcome visitor in the home except when they take up residence in the toilet!

Powerful owls nesting

Field Notes:

Owls need a large territory and like to nest in hollows, preferably in trees that are at least 200 years old.

WHERE: south-east Australia (New South Wales, Victoria and Queensland)

WHEN: owls stake out their territory and pair up during March and April.

WHAT TO LOOK OUT FOR: From the ground, you'll see a white chest covered with brown v-shaped markings and stripes under the tail.

In April, the south-east forests are full of the love-hungry hoots of Australia's largest owl — the Powerful Owl.

If you're out in the bush around autumn time, you might be lucky enough to hear the slow, deep 'hoot-hooot!' of the Powerful Owl. Chances are, this winter-breeding owl will be defending his territory as he prepares to find a mate and establish a nest.

Powerful Owls, the largest of all Australian owls, are fearsome predators and the worst nightmare of their favourite food: sugar gliders, and ringtail and brush-tail possums. Unseen and unheard, the winged hunter swoops onto an unwary possum, grasping it with its claws and breaking its neck. In one great bite, the Powerful Owl can eat a whole possum head! Over the course of a year, one owl can devour up to 350 possums. They also eat magpies, ravens and even white cockatoos.

Growing up to 65 centimetres long, the Powerful Owl looks very grand as it flaps slowly through the forest on enormous wings. They lay two round white eggs that are incubated for just over a month. When the eggs hatch, the mother sits on them while the father is kept busy feeding the whole family for several months. The chicks leave the nest around September, when you can often see the whole family roosting close together on a branch.

Powerful Owls nest in tree hollows, so they need to live in forests with very old trees that have lost their branches. These types of mature forests are becoming rare, and the owls may have trouble finding the right kinds of nesting holes in future.

Turtles go walkabout

They suck up water through their bottoms, squirt foul smelling liquid and live happily in raw sewage. Australian Freshwater (or Longneck) Turtles are tough, resilient creatures, armed with a battery of defences that enable them to take drought, pollution and even car accidents in their very slow stride.

The Freshwater Turtle can be recognised by its dark brown or black shell, with a creamy underside. As it gets older, the edge of its shell curls upwards and continues until the shell resembles a bowler hat when the turtle reaches old age. The turtle also has a very long neck which, when extended, makes the body half as long again. Freshwater Turtles can live up to 70 years old and weigh up to 1.5 kilograms.

At this time of year, especially if there's autumn rain, turtles like to climb out of their ponds and go walkabout to find food, strolling along at about a kilometre a day. Sometimes they can be seen wandering along the side or even in the middle of the road. But be warned! If you pick one up, it may squirt out a disgusting smelling liquid, a cross between the smell of rotten cabbage and a sewage treatment plant. It's really awful, especially in the car!

This smelly liquid comes from glands situated above each leg of the turtle. The liquid contains six different types of acids, making the Freshwater Turtle the most stinking turtle of all. But if you want to keep one as a pet, as many people do, don't worry too much. These turtles only stink if they get scared. If they are happy, they don't usually smell!

Field Notes:

True turtles have webbed feet for swimming, whereas tortoises (like the giant ones from the Galapagos Islands) have stumpy solid feet for walking on land.

WHERE: Many rivers in Victoria, New South Wales and Queensland, including the Murray-Darling system.

WHEN: March and April, turtles often leave their homes to search for food.

WHAT TO LOOK OUT FOR: Freshwater turtles prefer slow-moving ponds and rivers where insects and crustaceans are easier to catch.

© David Nelson

Longneck turtles look cute but be careful if you pick one up: you could get a smelly surprise.

King of all tides

Field Notes:

Be careful if you are on the beach during a King Tide. When the water comes in it's really moving fast and you might need to make a run for it!

WHERE: far north Queensland, north-west Western Australia

WHEN: In north Queensland: December to February and June to August; and in Western Australia: March and April. The big tides occur during the full and new phases of the Moon.

WHAT TO LOOK OUT FOR: At low tide, a huge expanse of sand and no sea in sight. At high tide, seawater covers the main street.

When the tide comes in in northern Australia, it just keeps coming in, and in, and in . . .

On a few nights each year, the beaches around northern Australia are inundated with massive high tides. These enormous surges, called King Tides, can be so big that they flood the streets of cities like Cairns, and cover playing fields with seawater. Yet a few hours later when the tide goes out, sometimes tens of kilometres, it looks like the whole ocean is empty.

In the West Australian town of Derby, they are proud of their King Tides and even celebrate with the Derby King Tide Day Festival. As part of the festival, the locals play the annual Derby mud football match. It's great fun to watch them playing in knee-deep seawater that has invaded the town's football field. In Cairns they even go 'street fishing', where a line is thrown into the seawater that has covered the local streets.

Derby's tides, which peak at 11.8 metres, are the second biggest in the world. They are beaten only by the 15-metre tides achieved in Nova Scotia, Canada. At the other end of the scale are the teeny tides of the Mediterranean, which peak at a weeny two to three centimetres.

King Tides are caused by a combination of the shape of the coastline and the influence of the Moon. The coast around Derby is a wide shallow bay. When the tide moves in from the deep ocean, the huge volume of water is squeezed in and up to fit into this bay. This effect is enhanced by the gravitational pull of the Moon, which causes the oceans to 'bulge' slightly around the Earth's equator.

Tassie Devils mating

If you're camping in the forests of Tasmania at this time of the year, prepare to be woken in the middle of the night by a blood-curdling scream! But don't worry. It's not a ghost or a murderer, just the raucous mating call of the Tasmanian Devil. April is mating season for Tassie Devils and they can make some pretty scary noises as they woo each other and defend their territory. When they are angry, their pink ears even turn purple!

After a few weeks of frenzied mating, the female gives birth to up to 40 tiny babies, which crawl into her backward-facing pouch and attach to her nipples. Here they stay warm and cosy during winter, growing quickly on their mother's rich milk.

Once they leave the pouch, the pups stay in a den under a log or in a cave, watched over by their mother until they are ready to tackle the big world alone. When the young animals emerge and spread out on their own, the population swells to such an extent it looks like a plague.

Tasmanian Devils are sometimes confused with the extinct Tasmanian Tiger, but this animal was wolf-sized and had stripes, whereas the wombat-sized Tassie Devil is covered in glossy blue-black fur with a white patch on its rump. They tend to be scavengers, preferring a nice rotten wallaby carcass to a live lamb. Their bite is 10 times as powerful as a dog's, and their amazingly powerful jaws crunch easily into bone. Sometimes, at the end of the feast, all that's left of the carcass are the teeth!

Field Notes:

Tasmanian Devils are usually solitary animals, except during mating season. Their call ranges from a few soft barks to a barrage of howling screams.

WHEN: April is mating season with pups born in May and June.

WHERE: Tasmania (and mainland Australia until a few thousand years ago).

WHAT TO LOOK OUT FOR: Footprints are an unusual square shape. Droppings are grey and full of bones.

© Paul Willis

More of a friend than a foe to farmers, the Tasmanian Devil prefers dead carcasses to live lambs.

Silvereyes migrate

Field Notes:

Silvereyes are easy to spot in summer when they come together in large flocks. They are the size of a sparrow and can be identified from a distance by the white ring around their eyes. You'll often see them in the garden, obligingly picking insects off your plants and eating them.

WHEN: April, May

WHERE: Tasmania to New South Wales, Queensland and South Australia

WHAT TO LOOK OUT FOR:

tiny sparrow-sized bird with white eye ring

© Paul Willis

Tiny silvereyes manage to find their way from Tasmania to Queensland each year without a map or compass.

Every April and May, a tiny 10-gram bird flies a migratory route from Tasmania to north Queensland. While this doesn't sound like a great distance, it's the equivalent of a human being swimming from New Zealand to Sydney, and then walking to Egypt!

This tough little bird is the silvereye, so called because of the white ring around its eye that makes it look like it's wearing wire-rimmed glasses.

Near Murwillumbah in far north New South Wales, a silvereye was once banded and then later recaptured near Devonport in Tasmania, proving it had flown a massive 1,600 kilometres!

Silvereyes navigate in a number of ways. For example, they can read the magnetic field of the Earth and take their bearings from the rising and setting sun. A pair of Tasmanian silvereyes was caught in the same Sydney garden three times in four years, which suggests that these birds follow very exact migration paths year after year. And as silvereyes can live up to 12 years old, they also learn and remember key landmarks in their migration journey.

It seems incredible that they bother migrating at all because there's plenty of food back home in Tasmania. But it's possible that the silvereye migration evolved a long time ago when Tasmania was still joined to the southern part of the Australian coastline. Such a migration would have been far less hazardous then, but because the migration is now hard wired into their brains, silvereyes still pack their bags and do the big trip every year.

Winter-flowering gums

Most gum trees in Australia flower in spring and summer, but the winter-flowering gums splash around their colourful blooms during the colder months. But there's one problem: winter is too cold for most of the insects that normally pollinate gum trees. Instead, winter-flowering gums, such as the Lemon-scented Gum, Yellow Gum and Flooded Gum must rely on birds and mammals.

Gliders and flying foxes are particularly important for pollination, as are parrots such as the Swift Parrot. But when birds and mammals are on the job, pollination can get pretty messy. Unlike insects, which delicately extract the pollen, birds and mammals just stick their head in the flower to suck up as much nectar as they can. Fortunately a fair bit of pollen also rubs off on their fur. As the animal continues to graze on other flowers, the pollen falls off and pollinates them. Here are some winter-flowering species in different areas:

Western Australia — Gungurru (*E.caesia*), Karri (*E.diversicolor*), and Ironbarks (*E.indurata*).

Northern Australia — Desert bloodwood (*E.terminalis*) and Long-fruited bloodwood (*E.polycarpa*).

Southern Qld / northern NSW — Narrow-leaved grey box (*E.pilligaensis*), Inland grey box (*E.microcarpa*) and Spotted gum (*E.maculata*).

Eastern Australia — Blue-leaved stringy bark (*E.agglomerata*), Narrow-leaved red ironbark (*E.crebra*) and the Tumbledown gum (*E.dealbata*).

South Australia — Blue gum (*E.leucoxylon*), and South Australian Mallee box (*E.porosa*)

Field Notes:

Eucalypts pollinated by birds and mammals tend to have brighter flowers than those species pollinated by insects. Look out for red, pink or orange-coloured blossoms and chances are a bird, possum or glider would enjoy feasting on it.

WHERE: Australia wide

WHEN: May to August

WHAT TO LOOK OUT FOR:

Fresh eucalypt flowers scattered on the ground during your winter bushwalks.

© Dean Nicolle

Winter-flowering gums brighten up the bush for us and provide a welcome meal for birds and marsupials.

Pygmy-possums hibernate

Field Notes:

When possums awake, they look for a mate and by December, mother possums will have up to four babies snuggled in a grass-lined nest.

WHEN: In March, April or May the possums start hibernating.

WHERE: The Victorian Alps at Mt Buller; between Mt Higginbotham and Mt Bogong; and in Mount Kosciuszko National Park.

WHAT TO LOOK OUT FOR:

It would be hard to see a pygmy-possum hibernating, but watch out in summer for their favourite food, Bogong moths.

© Linda Broome

Palm possum: the tiny Mountain Pygmy-possum weighs just a few hundred grams, yet survives sub-zero temperatures.

In America, where the winters are icy cold and thick with snow, many animals hibernate. But in Australia the seasons are much less extreme, so only one mammal takes a long winter snooze. This is the Mountain Pygmy-possum, a tiny marsupial that weighs less than a Mars bar, and which hibernates for up to seven months in a small area of the Victorian Alps. As Australians head down the slopes on their first winter ski run, this tiny possum may well be snoozing safely, metres below the surface.

For a long time it was thought that the Mountain Pygmy-possum was extinct. Then, in 1966, a male possum popped up in a university ski lodge at Mt Higginbotham in Victoria, very much alive. But these animals are still very rare; in fact the entire area where these possums are found in the wild only covers about eight square kilometres.

From May to October or November the possums sleep for up to 20 days at a time. Their body temperature drops to about 2°C. Then after a short break, they go straight back to sleep.

Hibernating allows the possums to save a lot of energy by not having to maintain the same body temperature as their surroundings. On top of the snow, temperatures can fall as low as -20°C, but snow is a good insulator, and the nests the possums build under rocks in the alpine boulder fields remain a snug 2°C.

So next time you're out skiing, don't shout too loud or you might wake a Mountain Pygmy-possum.

Stingless bees cool off

Did you know there is a type of bee that doesn't sting? What's more, it's native to Australia. The native stingless bee, or *Trigona*, looks a bit like a tiny black fly but instead of zipping off when you try and catch it, it will happily wander around on your hand with no fear at all.

That's the great thing about native bees — you can touch them without worrying about getting stung.

Stingless bees have sacs on their back legs, which become bright orange or yellow when stuffed full of pollen. The bees also collect nectar in their crop. Back at the hive, they ripen or dehydrate the nectar droplets by spinning them inside their mouthparts to make their own special honey. This honey tastes a bit like lemon sherbet and is quite delicious, although it's only produced in tiny amounts.

The bees' hive is spiral shaped, comprising of tiny individual pots made of plant resin, instead of a waxy comb. This makes it tricky for apiarists to get at the honey and collect it, but it can be done if you are very careful.

Native bee hives are often destroyed when land is cleared for agriculture and housing. But native bee enthusiasts in Queensland have formed a group to 'rescue' bees and find homes for them where they can live safely. Many people keep native bees in their backyards and find they not only pollinate the garden, but produce a lovely aroma of honey all year round. And you can order native bees through the post!

Field Notes:

In northern Australia, native bees are active all year round. In the southern parts of the country, they tend to hibernate in the cooler months.

WHEN: All year round

WHERE: Australia wide

WHAT TO LOOK OUT FOR:

Look carefully for small, black, fly-like insects foraging on grevilleas, banksias and other blossoms. They often feed side by side with the regular black-and-yellow honeybees.

© Peter Chew

Tiny native *Trigona* bees (small black insects, centre and right) forage side-by-side with an introduced honeybee.

Ant-loving butterflies

Field Notes:

If there are swarms of ants on a tree trunk, look closely to see if they are with large grubs many times their size. These are the butterfly larvae.

WHEN: All year round, depending on where.

WHERE: Tropical species breed all year, while more southerly species pass winter in egg, larval or pupal stage.

WHAT TO LOOK OUT FOR:

Adult butterflies flying in sunshine show brilliant flashes of iridescent green, blue, purple, bronze or orange.

Some ants look after butterflies instead of eating them. But the ants get something out of it too.

Traditionally mortal enemies, some Australian ants and butterflies have become the best of friends. In some species, ants tenderly care for butterfly larvae as if they were their own, even raising them in their own nests! About half of the group of butterflies known as the Lycaenids have evolved this very weird and special relationship with ants. They are easy to spot in the bush, being usually an iridescent purple, blue or copper on the upper wing surfaces.

The caterpillar of the rare and endangered Bathurst Copper Butterfly, for example, actually lives inside ant nests at the base of blackthorn trees. At night, the ants carry the butterfly larvae up the trunk to feed on the leaves and then bring them back down to the safety of the ant nest in the morning. After hatching, Lycaenid butterfly larvae look like slaters and may produce a loud clicking sound. This helps scare away predators.

But it's no free ride for the butterfly. When they are still caterpillars, before they metamorphose, they secrete sweet sticky syrup from glands on their body. The ants love this grub nectar, and that's why they are so keen to have the caterpillar come and stay.

Just to be on the safe side though, the caterpillar also secretes a chemical that makes it smell like an ant, fooling the ants into thinking it is one of them. But as soon as the grub turns into a butterfly, it looses its smell and must get out of the ant nest quickly or it will get eaten alive.

Corroboree Frogs' last dance

Australia has over 200 species of frogs, but one of the most amazing would have to be the Southern Corroboree Frog. Restricted to a small area of the Snowy Mountains in New South Wales, the frog is named for its startling colouration — brilliant yellow spots and stripes over black, like a painted warrior ready to dance.

Biologists believe that the frog's skin may be highly toxic, super charged with poisonous alkaloids it accumulates from a diet consisting mainly of ants. Perhaps the frog is making up in colouration for what it lacks in stature. Barely the size of a 20-cent coin, it is one of the tiniest frogs around and also very rare.

Until the 1970s, the squelching croak of this little frog was commonly heard around the bogs and ponds of the high alpine ranges. Then over just a few years, the waterways fell silent as the wild population of Corroboree Frogs took a nosedive. No one knows exactly why, but it's probably a combination of drought, fire and a deadly fungus called chytrid. The fungus was accidentally introduced into Australia from Africa in the 1930s and is responsible for the decline of many of our frogs.

The chytrid fungus attacks the proteins in frog skin. Because frogs partially breathe through their skin, the fungus eventually suffocates them. Frantic efforts are being made by frog experts to breed the Corroboree Frog in captivity but there has been no luck so far. While there are a good few thousand adults safely in captivity at the moment, there is barely a third of this number left in the wild.

Field Notes:

At this time of year, frogs and tadpoles are resting beneath a thick layer of snow, insulated from the worst of the cold.

WHERE: Mount Kosciusko National Park, New South Wales

WHEN: Corroboree frogs hibernate in winter and lay eggs in mid summer.

WHAT TO LOOK OUT FOR:

The call is a nasal grunt or a short, harsh squelching sound. The frogs are found in bogs and under logs.

© David Hunter

The gorgeous Corroboree Frog was once common in the Snowy Mountains but is now almost extinct.

Echidna trains

Field Notes:

Echidnas enjoy a diet of ants and termites, which they slurp up with their long sticky tongues.

WHERE: Australia wide

WHEN: Echidnas breed in winter.

WHAT To Look OUT FOR:

Echidnas form 'trains', walking around nose to tail for several weeks as a prelude to mating. Also check for circular trenches around trees made by echidna trains. The echidna's snout makes a small triangular hole when pressed into the ground.

© Barbara Smith

Echidnas like their solitude except around the winter mating season when they form a conga line of spines.

Normally it's a rare treat to see a spiny echidna snuffling along for ants by the side of the road. But at this time of the year, they are looking for a mate and the way they do this makes them far easier to spot in the bush. Instead of just pairing up, echidnas form 'trains' of up to ten individuals who walk around nose to tail for several weeks as a prelude to mating.

Scientists used to think these lines of echidnas were a family, with Dad at the front, Mum behind and then the kids. But it's been discovered that the lead echidna is actually a female and all her followers are males, keen to get to know her better. They jostle and shove each other out of the way until eventually only one is left. The female often walks round and round a tree followed by the male, forming a distinctive donut shape around the base of the trunk. When she's ready, mating can take place. This is a bit tricky because of the spines on their body, but echidnas manage it by lying on their sides facing each other, instead of one climbing on top of the other.

Echidnas are incredibly adaptable and one of the few Australian animals that can live in almost any habitat, from desert to snowy mountaintop. Being monotremes, they both lay eggs and suckle their babies, which are called 'puggles'. But this also means they have a low body temperature and a metabolism more like a reptile than a mammal. This is one way echidnas are able to adapt to different environments, and can even hibernate during hard times.

Brolgas dancing

One of our largest and most elegant water birds is the brolga, an animal legendary for the exotic dance it does during the mating season. Standing one and a half metres tall, brolgas are blue-grey or silver-grey with an unmistakable bright red head.

In June, brolgas in Australia's south are making their way to their breeding grounds. In the north they're heading out with their new chicks to join massive flocks. Brolgas pair up when quite young and stay with their partner for life, which is about seven years.

There are several Aboriginal legends about the dance of the brolga. One story tells of a young maiden who danced so much she turned into a brolga. The dance is an elaborate and stately affair. The bird begins by strutting, bobbing its head and then bowing, while it half opens its wings and shakes its whole body. A dancing brolga can leap up to a metre in the air, all the while flinging twigs and grass around it and making a loud trumpeting call.

But why do they do it? Bird experts once thought it was a courtship dance, and it's possible their performances may strengthen the bond between couples. They also dance to scare off predators such as foxes that like to eat their chicks. But brolgas also seem to dance for any reason at all. While researchers have long studied the brolga dance, we're no closer to understanding what it's all about. To find out exactly why brolgas dance, you'd have to ask a brolga!

Field Notes:

Brolgas prefer swamps, shallow lakes, flooded grasslands and salt marshes where they can feed on insects, seeds, shoots and bulbs.

WHERE: Across northern Australia and most of Queensland, New South Wales and Victoria. Brolgas are also found in Papua New Guinea.

WHEN: Flocks concentrate in the north during October and in the south from April to June.

WHAT TO LOOK OUT FOR:
A brolga is a very tall, greyish-blue bird with a bright red head.

© Matt Herring

Brolgas have an extraordinary mating dance that has inspired legends and mystified scientists.

Crow Butterflies gather

Field Notes:

Crow Butterflies have a slow and heavy flight.

WHERE: north and eastern Australia

WHEN: Large resting flocks appear in June and July.

WHAT TO LOOK OUT FOR:

The butterflies often rest in dead casuarina trees, paperbarks and rubber vines 1 6 metres above the ground. Full grown, the larva sports alternating bands of orange and black-edged with white along its body and eight pairs of black tentacles.

© Stephen Lin

The most spectacular winter aggregations of Common Crow Butterflies occur at lagoons and parks near Townsville, Cairns and Rockhampton.

Common Crow Butterflies have a neat trick for dealing with the dry winter weather. Around June or July, these large black-and-white butterflies gather in thousands and settle down among the trees. As the insects cluster together, it can be a spectacular seasonal sight in the bush.

Crow Butterflies survive the winter by remaining dormant — a behaviour called over-wintering. And they do it with lots of others of their kind because there's safety in numbers. If they can survive the winter, they will be able to breed when spring and the warmer weather arrives.

These butterflies can be found across northern and eastern Australia, preferring the coastal tropics, subtropics and cool gorges. One popular winter gathering spot is Katherine Gorge National Park in the Northern Territory. They have also adapted well to city life and even thrive on eating the leaves of the oleander, a poisonous plant to many other species. Crow Butterflies belong to a group of butterflies known as the danaines, nearly all of which contain poisonous compounds that make them unpalatable to birds and other predators. They derive these poisons from the milky sap of the oleander they like to eat. Once the predators taste one or two butterflies they quickly leave them alone!

The eggs from the butterflies are pale yellow and laid singly on the undersides of the leaves and flower buds. The grub (larva) is often spotted in the garden and easy to recognise, with its orange and black stripes and white edge along the body.

Winter wattles

If it weren't for winter-flowering wattles, the grey and green Australian bush would be a dull place in winter. Wattles are one of the few trees that flower during winter, providing a welcome source of nectar and pollen for hungry birds.

Up to a third of Australia's 960 species of wattle are winter flowerers and somewhere in Australia, no matter what time of year, a wattle is flowering. As the cool weather approaches, a tide of yellow sweeps down from the north and moves inland, the more southerly and inland species blooming later in the season than their northerly relatives.

The Acacia genus, which includes all the wattles, is the biggest group of trees and shrubs in Australia, topping even the eucalypts in diversity. They were part of the original Gondwana vegetation when Australia was joined to the other continents. This is why today acacias are also found in Africa, South America and India.

One of the best-known winter flowerers is the Cootamundra wattle. Although its pretty fern-like silver leaves make it popular with gardeners, it has become a pest in some areas. It can grow to be quite enormous and the seeds can survive for decades in the soil.

For many, a sprig of wattle has come to symbolise Australia. This goes back to the days when wattle was collected and sold to raise money for the war effort. These origins are still celebrated on National Wattle Day, the first day of spring, 1 September. The wattle also appears on the Commonwealth Coat of Arms, along with the emu and kangaroo.

Field Notes:

Bees go crazy for wattle blossom, which produces a strong fragrance and protein-laden pollen but very little nectar.

WHERE: Australia wide.

WHEN: Different wattles flower all year round, but many, unusually, flower during winter.

WHAT TO LOOK OUT FOR: Young wattles often have feathery leaves which become smooth and straight as they mature.

© Sue Lewty

Bees just can't resist the sweet clouds of nectar that float up from a winter wattle in full bloom.

Native truffles stinking

Field Notes:

Never eat truffles, as some are poisonous.

WHERE: Truffles can be found all over Australia and occupy a wide variety of habitats. They especially like the taller eucalypt forests of the south-east coast, but will also grow in the semi-arid interior.

WHEN: Truffles grow during mushroom season, from late autumn to spring.

WHAT TO LOOK OUT FOR: Animal diggings around a tree are a good sign that truffles grow there.

© Teresa Lebel

Some of the 250 known types of native truffles – they have a thin skin and are stuffed full of spore.

Next time you're out for a walk in the bush, don't be surprised to catch a whiff of bubblegum or even peanut butter. It might be someone's leftover picnic, but more likely there's a native truffle lurking nearby.

As winter approaches, these pungent underground fungi are ripe and ready for native animals to dig up and devour. Like their distant European cousin, the Australian truffle emits a strong odour. But while European truffles smell quite delicious, some Australian species can really stink, pumping out odours as diverse as petrol or rotting onions, road tar or even dog poo.

Australia has at least 250 species and perhaps up to 1,500 species of truffles living in just about every habitat from rainforest to mallee scrub. It's not unusual to find 10 different species of truffle living off the roots of a single big tree.

But while truffles might stink to us, native animals like bandicoots and potoroos just adore them. They dig them up and devour them, spreading the truffle spore (seed) around the forest in their poo. Potoroos eat up to 50 different species of truffles, and if these marsupials disappear from an area of bush, the truffles can no longer live there either. This can spell disaster for the trees in the area too, because under the ground truffles grow on the roots of trees. They transfer nutrients and water from the soil to the tree's roots and protect the roots from fungal diseases at the same time. For something that's so stinky and hard to find, truffles play a major role in keeping the Australian bush healthy.

Platypus look for love

In crystalline pools and burbling brooks at this time of year, male platypus are starting to patrol the river at high speed. Spurred on by the urge to breed, they leave little in their wake but a graceful bow wave as they race upstream to challenge intruder males or charm resident females into joining them in a sinuous mating dance.

Mating occurs in the water, with the male chasing and biting the tail of the female as they dive and twist under the water. Then the male wraps his body underneath the female while he grips her back with his bill and they interlock, still swirling around in the water. Males have poisonous spurs on their hind limbs that they use to duel with competing males. During the breeding season venom production is at its highest, and while it is rare for male platypus to die from their battle wounds, the toxin has been known to kill gun-dogs and can be extremely painful if injected into humans.

The female platypus excavates an extensive burrow, up to 30 metres long, and walls herself in with plugs of earth to protect against predators. She lays one to three leathery eggs that she incubates on her stomach for about ten days. After leaving the burrow, young platypus probably spend little time with their parents before heading off on their own. With such limited training and so much to learn, juveniles sometimes make mistakes, and they've been found living under busy six-lane highways, next to floodlit football fields and even in backyard swimming pools!

Field Notes:

Platypus float very low in the water, with only its head and rump visible.

WHERE: Eastern Australia from north Queensland to Tasmania, and introduced on Kangaroo Island.

WHEN: Breeding is from July to October, depending on location.

WHAT TO LOOK OUT FOR: Use binoculars to spot platypus at dawn and dust. Their diving creates a very distinctive circular ripple pattern.

Although they are elusive, there is a trick to spotting platypus in the wild: keep an eye out for ripples.

Magpies behaving badly

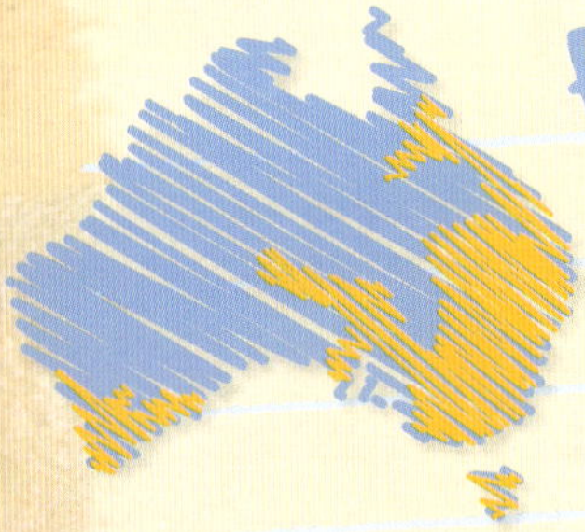

Field Notes:

Magpies are very intelligent, probably at the same level as parrots, and have very complex social systems.

WHERE: **New South Wales, Victoria, eastern South Australia, south-west Western Australia, coastal ranges of Queensland.**

WHEN: **Magpies begin breeding in July; chicks fledge in February.**

WHAT TO LOOK OUT FOR:

Magpies often dive-bomb you from behind or the side, swooping down from a high branch.

At this time of year be on the look out for magpies: they are defending their chicks.

In winter and early spring, it's time to scan the skies for a crazy black-and-white bundle of feathers, the Australian magpie. At this time of year magpies are feeding their chicks and while defending their young, they can be quite aggressive. About 80 per cent of respondents to a national survey a few years ago indicated magpies have attacked them. More men than women were attacked, and most birds went for the eyes.

In many areas, problem magpies are simply shot. But could magpies be getting a bad rap? When you delve deeper into their behaviour, it turns out that they are only aggressive for about six weeks a year, when the chicks are most vulnerable. Magpies tend to attack the same few individuals repeatedly, possibly because of a case of mistaken identity. Magpies are very intelligent and will remember the face of someone who once hurt them, even as a chick. Even if you wear different clothes, they can still recognise you.

Knowing more about magpies, there are some simple ways to deal with an attack. If you are on a bike or horse, get off immediately. Magpies feel much more threatened by a moving bike than a stationary one. If a particular bird keeps harassing you, go a different route for a few weeks until the chicks fledge. Magpies have an excellent memory and can tell the time and know exactly when a feared enemy is due to go past. And an old favourite that still works, even if it is a bit embarrassing: always wear an ice-cream container on your head when crossing magpie flight paths!

Dugongs on the move

Whales and dolphins are our most familiar sea mammals, but along side them, in the warmer waters of Australia, lives a far less common ocean dwelling mammal. This is the dugong, a large, slow-swimming creature with tiny eyes, a cute smile, four flippers and a tail like a whale. It's a large creature, up to three metres long and weighing as much as 400 kilograms. Yet being herbivorous, dugongs are not harmful to people.

During winter, dugongs may swim several hundreds of kilometres to warmer waters; one favourite spot is Fraser Island. Dugongs are more closely related to the hippopotamus and elephant than to the whale. In fact they are more of a giant aquatic cow, pottering along the bottom of the bay and munching seagrass as they go.

Dugongs have a homely face with a round head and a large, fleshy snout featuring prominent nostrils on the upper surface. They also have a coarse moustache of sensitive bristles covering the upper lip to help them find and grasp tender seagrass shoots. Unlike other marine mammals, dugongs cannot hold their breath for long and must regularly surface for air.

Dugongs can live for a long time — as much as 70 years — but breed slowly, only once every three to seven years. The mother is pregnant for between 13 and 15 months, then gives birth to a calf that suckles from a nipple in its mother's armpit. Because both mother and calf need to come up for air regularly, the mother occasionally rears out of the water, holding on to the suckling calf with her flipper so it can breathe too.

Field Notes:

Dugong numbers have declined dramatically along the Queensland coast in the last 40 years, as a result of boat strikes, hunting and fishing, pollution and shark nets.

WHERE: Along the north coast between Shark Bay in Western Australia and Moreton Bay in Queensland.

WHEN: Dugongs move to warmer waters during winter, from June to August.

WHAT TO LOOK OUT FOR:

Dugongs hang out in shallow, sandy bays with a rich growth of seagrass on the bottom.

© Great Barrier Reef Marine Park Authority

Like a giant aquatic cow, the enigmatic dugong grazes on seagrass in the warm tropical waters of Australia.

Soaring the Glory

Field Notes:

The Morning Glory forms over the Gulf of Carpentaria and moves in over land like a giant shockwave.

WHERE: From Burketown in Queensland and across the Gulf of Carpentaria.

WHEN: August to November

WHAT TO LOOK OUT FOR:

The Morning Glory is a massive backwards-rolling cloud formation up to 1,000 kilometres long and a kilometre high which can travel at speeds of up to 60 kph.

© Russell White

Each year, a few daredevil pilots attempt to surf the Morning Glory — a 1000-kilometre long rolling cloud formation.

There's one seasonal phenomenon in Australia that is strictly for thrill-seekers only. For a few brief months in late winter and spring, a small band of brave pilots bring their gliders and ultra-light aircraft to a special spot in far north Queensland for the experience of a lifetime.

They are seeking to surf or 'soar' the Morning Glory, a freakish travelling cloud up to 1,000 kilometres in length and one kilometre high. It rolls along like a giant steamroller reaching speeds of up to 60 kph. The Glory is created when easterly and westerly winds collide over Cape York, generating a huge travelling pressure wave.

To 'soar' the Morning Glory (soar is a term used by pilots to describe flying without the engine), you fly straight up towards it as it approaches you. When the plane comes into contact with the lower front edge of the cloud, the backward-rotating motion instantly lifts the aircraft straight up into the air. You can surf the cloud in this way, floating on the updraft with no need for an engine, for several hours. It takes nerves of steel as, perched inside a tiny fragile glider with the engine turned off, pilots expose themselves to forces which could crush them to fragments in an instant.

On a good day, the updraughts can thrust you 3,000 metres up into the sky and carry you hundreds of kilometres, with your aircraft reaching speeds of 150 kph. As the Glory runs out of steam, you cross your fingers and kick your engine over. Then it's time for the long flight back to safe ground.

Emu chicks hatch

Emus are winter breeders, which means that their chicks hatch in winter and spring. But the mating season starts long before this, back in mid-summer. To find a mate, emus go through some amazing courtship rituals. The birds fill their throat pouches with air to make a drumming sound, which can be heard hundreds of metres away. They fluff their feathers and dip their heads, grunting and bobbing around. The males also fight each other with powerful frontal kicks.

Mating begins around April and the female lays an egg every two or three days, producing a clutch of up to 20 eggs. Her job is now finished and Dad looks after the babies for the next 18 months. The eggs take eight weeks to hatch and during this time, Dad carefully turns them a dozen times a day to keep them evenly warm. When the cute stripy chicks hatch out, it is Dad who teaches them how to survive, leading them to feeding areas and showing them what to eat. Emu chicks grow very quickly, putting on a kilogram a week at first. They reach their full height at about a year old but don't breed until about 20 months.

White settlers in Australia used to hunt emus for their meat and oil. Outback housewives made omelettes from their eggs, which they first broke into a basin and let stand overnight so they could skim off the oil that rose to the top. Emu eggs weigh over half a kilogram, so if you want to make an emu omelette for the family, one is probably enough. One emu egg equals about 10 to 12 chicken eggs!

Field Notes:

Emus are good swimmers and they love the water. On a hot day they'll take a cool dip in the creek, dam, or even under the sprinkler.

WHERE: Most of inland Australia except rainforests and extreme desert.

WHEN: Emu chicks hatch from June to September.

WHAT TO LOOK OUT FOR: Emus prefer open pasture country. Look out for a tall skinny neck poking above the grass.

© Charm Venn

Baby emus look nothing like their parents but their stripes help prevent them from being seen by predators.

WA wildflowers show off

Field Notes:

Everlasting daisies that form yellow, pink or white carpets are most spectacular along the Great Eastern Highway and north and east of Geraldton.

WHERE: The western third of Western Australia.

WHEN: Most flowers appear from June to December with a peak in spring.

WHAT TO LOOK OUT FOR: Red and orange gum blossoms, orange banksias, pink boronias, red-and-green kangaroo-paw and magenta paperbarks.

© Michael Smith

Every spring, parts of Western Australia are carpeted with vivid wildflowers such as this Sturt's Desert Pea.

Wildflower season in Western Australia is legendary. People come from all over the world to witness the massive colourful displays of over 13,000 species, many of which start flowering in June and finish in December.

Despite being a dry and infertile environment, Western Australia has managed to produce some of the largest, most colourful and most spectacular flowers in the country. For sheer size and beauty, there are the kangaroo-paws, orange banksias, white proteas and the huge *Eucalyptus macrocarpa*, an enormous red blossom the size of a saucer. Carpets of brilliant everlasting daisies seem to stretch to the horizon.

How is it possible for such a barren landscape to be so productive? Well it's for precisely that reason: the tougher the conditions, the harder the plants must compete with each other for pollinators. This has driven an evolutionary trend towards bigger, better flowers, as if each plant is saying to local insects, birds or mammals: 'Pick me! Pick me!'

There is another reason why Western Australia wildflowers are so spectacular: the landscape is the oldest and most undisturbed in Australia. Not for several hundred million years have glaciers, volcanoes or even earthquakes disrupted the environment, leaving it at peace to evolve a truly amazing range of plants and animals.

The unique qualities of Western Australia have recently been recognised by Conservation International, with the inclusion of the south-west corner of the state among 25 biodiversity 'hotspots' on the planet.

Humpbacks migrating

Humpback Whales lead quite exotic lifestyles. During the summer they hang out in the cold Southern Oceans near Antarctica, feeding on the plentiful krill and plankton. Then as the weather cools down, Humpbacks migrate 12,000 kilometres northwards to spend winter and spring in the tropical waters off the coast of Queensland. This is when they calve. Around September is the best time to see Humpbacks travelling south with their newborn babies, back to their summer feeding grounds around Antarctica.

Newly arrived baby Humpback Whales are already the size of a big car! They can drink over 200 litres of milk a day from nipples hidden on their mother's belly. Young calves surface frequently for air but by adulthood they'll be able to stay underwater for as long as 45 minutes.

The best places for spotting whales and their calves are the headlands and islands along the east, south-west and west coasts of Australia. South-east Queensland and northern New South Wales are great for whale watching because the coastline bulges east making it more likely that the shore-hugging Humpbacks will come in close.

As whales go, Humpbacks are medium sized. They have two blowholes, while toothed whales such as Sperm Whales only have one. A Humpback's mouth is so big that it can take in 10,000 litres of water in a single gulp. It then uses its tongue to force the water out through the baleen, leaving behind the krill and plankton to munch on.

Field Notes:

Watch out for whale breath! Eating lots of plankton can give whales a bad case of fishy smelling halitosis, which you'll smell when they spurt air out of their blowhole.

WHERE: east and west coast of Australia.

WHEN: September and october

WHAT TO LOOK OUT FOR:

Humpbacks grow up to 18 metres long. They are black with white markings on the underside of their tails, flippers and dorsal fin. Each Humpback has a different shaped tail and this helps identify them.

During their migration, Humpback Whales come as close as 50 metres to the shore in spots like Hervey Bay in Queensland.

Killer ladybirds

Field Notes:

Ladybirds lay clusters of 20 to 50 yellow or orange eggs on the underside of leaves.

WHERE: Australia wide, depending on species

WHEN: All year round, but especially in early spring.

WHAT TO LOOK OUT FOR:

The ladybirds with the fewest spots tend to be the 'good' ones: those that eat insect pests rather than your vegies! Check for ladybirds under leaves, especially pumpkin.

In the old days, ladybirds were considered to be lucky and killing one would bring misfortune.

After hibernating all winter, brightly coloured ladybirds emerge in spring to feed and find a mate. Ladybirds are considered a sign of good luck in many cultures, and killing one is believed to bring misfortune. Why is that? It turns out that despite their cute appearance, ladybirds are lethal killers. Their favourite food are insect pests such as mealy bugs and aphids, which attack crops and vegetable gardens. They can be lured to any garden by offering them a mixture of honey, water and brewer's yeast.

Ladybirds do such a great job cleaning up pests that they are sometimes released onto crops instead of spraying insecticides. The larvae of the Mealy Bug Ladybird, for example, feed off the eggs of the mealy bug, a serious insect pest. So effective are they that 500 of these ladybirds were introduced into California in the early 1900s to save the citrus industry from pest attack.

Ladybird larvae are bizarre looking earwig-like creatures with huge jaws that can chomp up to 100 aphids a week. But some ladybirds are less popular with farmers, for example, the 28-Spotted Ladybird, feeds on tomato, pumpkin and potato plants. To defend themselves, ladybirds ooze a noxious liquid from their leg joints, which deters other insects from eating them. Ladybirds have even been sent into space on a NASA space shuttle to see if they could control pests in space-station vegetable gardens. To the delight of astronauts, the ladybirds thrived, assuring them of a future place on the first human colony in space!

What scat is that?

Scats are another name for animal poo or droppings. They come in all shapes, sizes, textures and colours, and they're a great way to identify animals.

Wombat poo, for example, comes in a very distinctive cube shape, about two centimetres wide, and is one of the easiest scats to identify. They are usually left on rocks and steps, apparently because wombats like to wipe their bums!

Possums generally produce strong-smelling, cylindrical scats that may contain leaves.

Kangaroo and wallaby scats are often found in grassy places such as a big paddock. Kangaroos have small, round, black scats and usually leave several in the same place. They are very similar to wallaby poos, but larger. Wallaby scats are pointier than kangaroo scats and sometimes have fibres sticking out. The black outer covering conceals a dry, yellowy, grassy matrix inside.

Koalas have a distinctive poo that is very hard on the outside, and has a slightly ridged and oval shape. Fox scats look just like the poo left by small dogs and smell terrible.

Even if you don't know which animal the scat came from, you can do a bit of detective work to find out the species. If the scat is fairly dry, break it open and have a look inside. If it's a kangaroo or other macropod, chances are it contains finely chopped bits of grass. If it's a cat, fox, Tasmanian Devil or other carnivore, the scat will probably contain hair and bits of bone. The most common scats found are from possums, eastern grey kangaroos, swamp wallabies and other macropods.

Field Notes:

The bigger the animal, the larger the scat it leaves.

WHERE: Australia wide, including beaches and oceans.

WHEN: As spring approaches, animals become more active and leave plenty of scats behind.

WHAT TO LOOK OUT FOR:
All animals leave scats, even snakes, birds, lizards, whales and insects. Start looking for them and you'll find scats everywhere. Wombat scats are common and easy enough to recognise because they are cube-shaped.

© Paul Willis

This scat contains hairs and bits of bone, suggesting it came from a Tasmanian Devil.

Corals spawning

Field Notes:

In the branching corals the eggs take about nine months to develop and the sperm about three to four months.

WHERE: Great Barrier Reef, Queensland and Ningaloo Reef, Western Australia

WHEN: October to December (GBR); March and April (Ningaloo).

WHAT TO LOOK OUT FOR:
Thick clouds of pink bubbles or milky streams coming out of corals. This pink slick sometimes washes up on beaches or rocks.

When corals spawn, they release millions of tiny pink eggs and sperm into the sea.

When the Moon is just past full and the water temperature is rising, it's time for corals on the Great Barrier Reef to start spawning. Each tiny coral polyp ejects an egg and a sperm, and the combined effect of millions of polyps doing this at the same time is like a pink underwater snowstorm. The tiny eggs and sperm are like champagne bubbles, filling the water with a pink cloud that rises to the surface and forms an oily, strong-smelling slick that can stretch for kilometres. Sometimes these slicks are so big that satellites orbiting the Earth can see them!

The spawn slicks can also kill fish and coral because they remove oxygen from the water as the eggs and sperm rot down. If the corals spawn at low tide on a warm day, they can leave thick rafts of the pink egg-and-sperm 'soup' sitting high and dry on the reef shelf. When the eggs and sperm are released, the eggs float to the surface and the sperm swims around looking for eggs to fertilise. As soon as an egg is fertilised, it becomes a tiny free-swimming creature for a few days, before attaching itself to a rock and growing into an adult coral.

Researchers have become more interested in coral spawning since the death of many corals from warmer waters associated with global warming. If the spawn can be harvested, they could be used to seed areas of the reef where coral has died and help bring it back to life. This may buy some time but it does depend on having healthy coral nearby to provide eggs and sperm.

cockatoos attack!

Sulphur-crested Cockatoos are a familiar sight these days, not just out in the bush, but hanging around the coastal cities of Australia. Until the 1960s these large white parrots hardly ever ventured over the mountain ranges to the coast, but that's all changed now. Rumour has it that a few decades ago a bird trapper released hundreds of birds in Sydney and they've bred up into thousands. Many have also escaped from captivity, and the abundant food sources associated with human settlements means that many cockatoos are now permanent city slickers.

Although cockatoos are spectacular and beautiful birds, they can also create problems. In spring, the adults are looking for nest sites. Once they made hollows in trees, but now they are more than willing to chew a nest in someone's timber roof, deck or wall! Houses made of western red cedar are a special favourite of cockatoos because the timber is soft and easy to chew. Some homes made of this wood have nearly been destroyed by hundreds of aggressive cockies.

After the spring rush, there's often another assault in autumn, when young cockatoos leave the nest. They are even more curious than their parents and will happily chew on any fence, roof, gate or trellis just to find out how much damage they can do! Why do they do it? Certainly cockies do a lot of chewing to keep healthy – their beaks never stop growing so they need to gnaw on something hard to keep the beak trimmed down. Others believe that these highly intelligent birds do it because they are bored, or simply just for fun!

Field Notes:

Eats seeds, insect larvae and berries (and your roof!).

WHERE: coastal Australia

WHEN: Most attacks on houses and trees happen in spring and autumn.

WHAT TO LOOK OUT FOR: Bright yellow crest, white body, loud raucous screech. The flight of the cockatoo is an uneven pattern of flap-flap-glide, and they sometimes swoop down just before landing. They grow to about 50 centimetres long.

© Alan Kwok

Structures built of red cedar are a favourite target for the marauding beaks of Sulphur-crested Cockatoos.

Malleefowls nesting

Field Notes:

Malleefowls were once plentiful, but habitat loss has reduced them to half their previous range.

WHERE: Mallee country of New South Wales, Victoria, Western Australian and South Australia

WHEN: October

WHAT TO LOOK OUT FOR:

A one-metre high volcano-shaped mound of red dirt filled with leaves. These mounds are built in mallee country, a type of arid and semi-arid forest dominated by mallee eucalypts.

© David Priddel

Malleefowls form long bonds, probably for life, and each pair occupies a permanent territory.

Out in the mallee country a little Aussie bird is doing the impossible. It's shifting literally tons of dirt, all in the name of making babies. The malleefowl believes that 'big is best' and it builds an enormous nest that looks like a miniature volcano up to one metre high and 12 metres across. That's a lot of nest for a bird the size of a big chicken!

From October to December, the female malleefowl lays one egg every week or so into the mound. It takes a week to form the next egg, because each egg weighs a massive one-tenth of her whole body. The big pile of dirt acts as an incubator, keeping the eggs warm until they hatch.

To make sure the temperature stays just right, the male malleefowl rushes around removing dirt or piling it on again, depending on whether the mound needs to be cooled or heated. In the morning he might dig the soil away and spread it out to be warmed by the sun. Once it's warm he works furiously to return the sand to the mound. The eggs need to stay at around 33°C. To keep a check on this, the male makes a small hole in the mound, sticks his whole head in and tests the soil with his tongue! Despite all this attention, once the chicks hatch (taking up to 15 hours to dig their way out) they are totally on their own and receive no parental care at all.

The malleefowl's habitat is fast disappearing though, with much of our original mallee country now cleared to grow wheat and graze sheep.

Bellowing koalas

They might look passive and sleepy, but come mating time, koalas turn into noisy and aggressive creatures that you'd never want to cuddle in a million years. Male koalas are very territorial, and the larger individuals command an area of up to 1.5 hectares. As spring breeding season approaches, the male patrols his trees in search of females who are ready to mate. The action really starts if he spots another male hanging out in his territory.

First he tries to scare off the intruder with a loud, harsh bellow. It's a weird and spine-chilling call, a bit like water gurgling down the drain followed by a log being hacked up with a really blunt saw. If this doesn't work, the big guy moves in for the attack and he's not interested in playing fair. The male initially rushes up to attack the second koala, which either retreats to the end of the branch or races past the attacker and down the tree. If the attacker manages to reach the other koala, he thrusts one arm around his opponent's shoulders and bites his elbow, often causing deep wounds. Sometimes he even pulls the intruder right out of the tree.

Because these encounters need a lot of strength and experience, most male koalas don't get to mate with a female before they turn four or five. Males aren't the only ones to voice their feelings: female koalas can also snarl or scream if they feel threatened. But whereas the males specialise in terrifying howls, females spend most of their time murmuring, squeaking and clicking quietly to their baby, much truer to the cuddly image we have of koalas!

Field Notes:

Koalas in the southern parts of Australia have longer, shaggier fur than those which live in the north.

WHERE: East coast, from far north Queensland to Victoria and coastal South Australia. Inhabit tall coastal eucalypt forests, but not rainforest or desert.

WHEN: Mating runs from August to February.

WHAT TO LOOK OUT FOR:

Koalas have two thumbs on each paw to help them hang on to the tree branch while they eat.

© Dick Marks, Australian Koala Foundation

Like kangaroos, baby koalas are called joeys, and will stay with their mother for up to a year.

Quolls quit the pouch

Field Notes:

Most common in the dry eastern half of Tasmania at low to medium altitudes.

WHERE: Tasmania

WHEN: November

WHAT TO LOOK OUT FOR:

often found where bushland meets pasture, hunting for grubs and beetles. They are agile and nimble enough to scamper up trees as they search for food but will retreat into a hollow log if frightened.

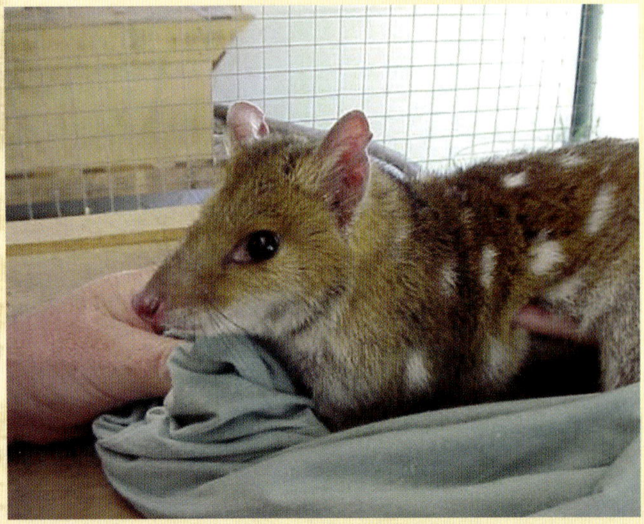

© Abbie Thomas

This Eastern Quoll is part of an endangered species breeding program at Lithgow, New South Wales.

Eastern Quolls once lived across New South Wales, Victoria and South Australia but are now probably extinct on the mainland. Tasmania is their only remaining home. Other quolls that survive on the mainland are the Spotted Quoll, Northern Quoll and Western Quoll.

Around this time of year, young Eastern Quolls have abandoned their mother's pouch and started their own life. After three months tucked up in the pouch, they are full of curiosity and want to explore. If you are out in the Tasmanian bush, you might see young quolls playing together at night and chasing each other's tails. Eastern Quolls are cat-sized, with large dark eyes, a bright red wet nose and fawn or black coat spattered with white spots. They are very agile and are as much at home climbing a tree as scampering across the ground.

Mainly insect-eaters, quolls also scavenge carcasses, eat seasonal fruits such as blackberries and enjoy the occasional lizard snack. They became extinct on the mainland for several reasons: they were frequently shot because it was thought they stole chickens, and then almost wiped out by a mysterious disease in the 1800s. Cats and foxes probably cleaned up the last few survivors. Thankfully Eastern Quolls still flourish in Tasmania today. If it ever became legal to keep a native animal as a pet, Eastern Quolls would be a top choice. Those who have lived with them say they willingly co-habit with cats, love cuddles and can even use kitty litter.

Bogong moths fly south

Early summer barbeques along the east coast of Australia wouldn't be the same without a visit from a flock of Bogong moths. Millions of these chubby brown moths migrate south every year, travelling more than 1,000 kilometres from Queensland and western New South Wales to the Australian Alps.

Bogong moths usually travel by night but if they see a light or fire below, they immediately fly towards it. Some people believe this is because moths think any light is the Moon, and they use the Moon to navigate by. So in early summer you may find Bogong moths flying around your veranda light, around street lamps or even doing a kamikaze into the flames of your barbeque! One particular star-struck moth was attracted to the brilliant lights coming from the closing ceremony of the Sydney Olympic Games. As millions watched around the world, it attached itself firmly to the dress of singer Yvonne Kenny and didn't budge during her entire performance.

As the moths rest up in the cool caves over summer, they form an essential part of the diet of the tiny Mountain Pygmy-possum (see page 20). Aboriginal people living in alpine areas also depended on this annual bonus of food. Bogong moths were considered a delicacy, with their wings singed off by the fire and their plump juicy bodies roasted in the coals. Local people still celebrate the arrival of the moth with the Ngan Girra (Bogong moth) Festival, held near Albury every year on the last Saturday in November. Here you can sample Bogong moth dishes such as bogong damper and even a mothy version of popcorn, called 'Popmoth'.

Field Notes:

Bogongs travel by night and drop down to the ground to rest in the shade during the day.

WHERE: Darling Downs, Queensland; Bogong Plains, Victoria (near Mt Beauty)

WHEN: Bogong moths fly south in spring and return to Queensland in autumn to mate and die.

WHAT TO LOOK OUT FOR: The brown mottled wings are about five centimetres and each one has two light-coloured spots.

© Linda Broome

To escape the summer heat, Bogong moths gather in thousands in the cool caves of the Australian Alps.

Grasshoppers on show

Field Notes:

You'll need to make a stiff hike up into the sandstone plateaus of Kakadu National Park to spot this grasshopper.

WHERE: occurs in small, isolated populations in Kakadu National Park, Katherine, and Keep River National Park.

WHEN: Emerge as adults in November.

WHAT TO LOOK OUT FOR:
orange or red wings with black spots, and a brilliant blue saddle behind the head. Often found on Pityrodia, a small, aromatic bush.

© Lyn Lowe

Leichhardt's Grasshopper was thought to be extinct for 120 years but reappeared in 1973 during mining explorations.

Australia is home to one of the world's most spectacular grasshoppers — the Leichhardt's Grasshopper. It comes dressed up in a brilliant outfit of red, blue and orange and is by far our most colourful grasshopper. These exotic markings are meant to warn predators that this insect tastes bad.

Leichhardt's Grasshopper is found around Darwin and Arnhem Land in the Northern Territory, where the local people call it 'Alyurr', meaning 'children of the Lightning Man'. This Lightning Man was a powerful ancestral being and there are many rock paintings showing him with antennae sticking out of his head, just like a grasshopper. The grasshoppers live in what the locals call 'stone country', huge sandstone plateaus that rise several hundred metres out of the surrounding plains.

Despite their brilliant appearance, Leichhardt's Grasshoppers are picky eaters, preferring just one type of plant — a sticky aromatic bush called Pityrodia. A grasshopper may spend its entire life on just one bush, going through seven moults from egg to full grown adult.

The nymphs look like tiny grasshoppers and grow very slowly until about August when the weather gets warmer and things start to speed up. In September/October the grasshoppers begin to get more colourful and around November, they emerge from their final moult in full adult splendour. Mating happens around Christmas and the eggs lay in wet sand during January and February. Then their bodily systems slow down and the grasshoppers literally fall off the twig and can be found dead around the base of their home plant.

Blue-ringed octopus hatch out

At first you feel nothing. Then after a few minutes, your lips and tongue go numb. You start to have trouble breathing. You can't move or respond when your name is called, even though you can hear everything that's going on around you! This is what it's like to be bitten by a Blue-ringed Octopus — the tiniest and most deadly octopus in the world.

People can recover if bitten by a Blue-ringed Octopus, but only if they seek immediate medical attention. Of course the best strategy is to avoid contact with the octopus altogether. There is no antidote to the toxin, which is the same as that found in the puffer fish. Each golf-ball sized octopus contains enough poison to paralyse an adult.

During early summer swimming, it's important to stay alert for these tiny, elegant creatures, which spend much of their time around rock pools and under ledges, close to shore. The eggs are beginning to hatch now after being carried around for several months tucked snugly under the arms of the mother octopus. When the baby octopus emerges, it looks like a tiny adult and drops to the bottom.

At rest, the adult Blue-ringed Octopus is an unimpressive grey with brown patches. But if disturbed or trodden on, it lights up to a brilliant yellow and the trademark blue spots appear, glowing iridescently across the body. It's an unmistakable warning that everyone should be able to recognise. Despite this, the Blue-ringed Octopus is popular with aquarium owners, because it doesn't possess an ink sac and so can't mess up the water. Enthusiasts frequently have no idea of the danger that lurks in their tank!

Field Notes:

There are seven species of Blue-ringed octopus in Australia, the most common of which are the Lesser and Greater Blue-ringed octopus.

WHERE: The Lesser Blue-ringed octopus is found in southern waters from southern Western Australia around to Tasmania and southern Queensland and New South Wales. Other species live further north and up into Indonesia.

WHEN: Eggs hatch in spring and early summer.

WHAT TO LOOK OUT FOR: Golf-ball sized grey or brown octopus, lurking under a rock or ledge. Avoid touching or annoying in any way.

© Mark Norman

You'd never guess a small, boring-looking, grey-and-brown octopus could transform into this brilliant creature when disturbed.

Top End lightning show

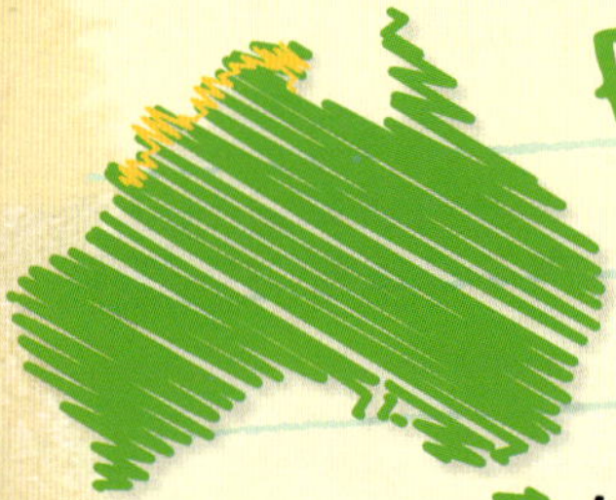

Field Notes:

The local Aboriginal people had a fiery Dreamtime spirit called the Lighting Man. There are cave paintings of him at Kakadu, carrying a lightning bolt across his shoulders and wielding stone axes for creating thunder.

WHERE: Northern Territory, Western Australia

WHEN: summer

WHAT TO LOOK OUT FOR:

In the most severe and destructive storms, the lightning will be seen to leap from one cloud to another, rather than from cloud to ground.

Lightning can strike more than once in the same place, especially in Australia's Top End during summer.

As Christmas approaches, people living in northern Australia say they go a bit 'troppo' or crazy, as the heat and humidity builds up towards the wet season. When the storms finally break, the tropical north is treated to some of the most spectacular lightning shows in the world.

One summer, a single thunderstorm over Darwin produced an incredible 1,634 lightning flashes in just a few hours. Perth only gets this much lightning in an entire year. For the first few months of the wet season, there is lightning most nights, and about 40 per cent of all electricity blackouts are caused by lightning. Burn marks frequently appear on local power poles and other tall structures.

Why is Darwin such a magnet for lightning? It starts with a hot day, when the sun heats up the ground and causes the air to rise. As this moist air travels upwards, it cools and forms ice crystals. When these crystals collide inside a cloud, they become electrically charged. When they discharge their electrons we see a bolt of lightning.

Lightning can be beautiful but deadly. It accounts for between five to ten deaths a year in Australia. This figure is likely to go up as more people take up outdoor sports and travel more in the bush. Even so, most injuries still happen inside, especially when people use their home phone during a thunderstorm. The phone system becomes highly charged and can cause burns or even electrocution to the user. So during a thunderstorm, it's better to leave the calls for later and go sit near a window and enjoy the light show.

Cassowary dads patrolling

Cassowaries are large, tropical, emu-sized birds with a black body, blue neck and a huge crest on the head. Like emus they are one of very few birds where the male raises the chicks. But while male emus nest all together, each male cassowary has to do it on his own.

After a female lays her eggs directly onto the forest floor, father cassowary takes over. He sits on the eggs (each weighing half a kilogram) for 50 days, barely eating or drinking. After the chicks hatch in spring, they stick with their father for up to 18 months.

At first the chicks just eat insects, but pretty soon they learn to eat fruit, with their father teaching them which plants are good and which to avoid. He might do this by picking up a fruit and then clicking it in his beak. Having got the chicks' attention, he drops the fruit and they run over and eat it. While the chicks are very small, the father often breaks large fruit up to make it easier for them to eat. Cassowaries devour 150 different types of forest fruits, and so are very important for spreading seed around and regenerating the forest.

But cassowaries have also learnt to like the food we enjoy, and it is not uncommon for them to hang around roadsides and picnic areas in far north Queensland, waiting to steal a sandwich or a meat pie. Tragically, many cassowaries are killed on the roads this way and no amount of their father's protection can save them from this fate. Visitors to the wet tropics are now encouraged not to feed cassowaries, so that they are left to find their own wild food and stay safely away from roads.

Field Notes:

Once wide-spread, about 1,500 cassowaries still exist in the wild; this is less than the number of pandas still living in the forests of China.

WHERE: The wet tropics (including the Daintree Rainforest) and Cape York in Queensland.

WHEN: Cassowaries nest from October onwards.

WHAT TO LOOK OUT FOR:

Cassowaries stand up to 1.8 metres tall. Their call is a deep booming or coughing and the chicks make a whistling sound.

© Mark Hinder

They are supposed to eat native fruits, but cassowaries also adore sandwiches, pies and even chilli con carne!

Summer beetles

Field Notes:

Some insects are now protected so it's best not to take them home if you are not sure. The adults often only live a few weeks and should be left alone right now because this is the time of year when they are mating.

WHERE: Australia wide

WHEN: December to February

WHAT TO LOOK OUT FOR:

Beetle hunting is best done at night. Look around the lights of verandas, toilet blocks, service stations, tennis courts and street lamps.

© Angus Hawke

This friendly chap belongs to the diverse group known as the weevils, Australia's largest family of beetles.

Beetles just love the warm weather that summer brings and at this time of year you'll find them out chewing leaves and laying their eggs. Australia might have up to 80,000 species of beetle (there are many yet to be discovered), and the Sydney area alone is probably home to about 1,500 species.

Beetles, which are classified as insects because they have six legs, have managed to colonise almost every type of habitat — from deep caves to flowing rivers and right up to the treetops. You'll find most beetles stay around until February, when they mate, lay eggs and die. However, some beetles, such as the spectacular Rhinoceros beetle live for more than a year, making it a good pet.

Some of the best-known and easily found beetles are the scarabs (these include the Christmas beetles and Rhinoceros beetles), fireflies, Jewel beetles, water beetles, weevils, Longicorns, lady beetles, rove beetles, dung and carrion beetles, click beetles, leaf chewers and chafers.

The beetle world is full of surprises. Fireflies, for example, are not flies at all but actually beetles; and male Rhinoceros beetles use their antlers to push each other out of trees during mating season. Water beetles can fly long distances in search of water and are fearsome predators: their larvae have huge jaws which can pierce a tadpole or small fish and suck out its guts, while adult water beetles squirt a chemical into the water which paralyses its prey. Jewel beetles are brilliantly coloured but so attracted to bright shiny things that males often mate with beer bottles by the side of the road, mistaking them for females!

Pythons join the rat race

As the December rains begin to fall in tropical northern Australia, one of the world's strangest migrations takes place. Native dusky rats, which live on the flood plains during the dry season, are forced by rising waters to seek higher ground. But as they make their way up into the hills, they are quietly followed by thousands of sleek green water pythons. It's the only place in the world where pythons follow rats in such a seasonal way.

The pythons have no choice but to follow — dusky rats make up 95 per cent of their diet. These reptiles are superbly adapted to eating a 20-centimetre rat whole — the python's upper jaw is not fused to the skull and its jawbones are only loosely joined. So they can spread their bones apart and slide a rat into their mouth without even having to chew it up.

By day both rats and water pythons lie hidden, emerging at night to look for food. The python has special pits in either side of its lips that can detect the warmth of a nearby animal, even in the dark. This is what helps it find its prey. A python can also 'smell' a rat with its flicking tongue. Then it's just a matter of grabbing the rat and slowly swallowing it. A single rat can keep a python going for a long time.

Although it's a sad end for the rat, the population is in no danger. Dusky rats can have up to 12 babies at a time and start breeding from the age of seven weeks. Then they can produce a litter every three weeks! Perhaps it's just as well we have water pythons to keep the rats from taking over.

Field Notes:

The Top End floodplains have the highest density of animals in the world. If you spread all the rats out evenly, there'd be one every ten square metres.

WHERE: The Kimberley, Northern Territory and tropical parts of Queensland, north of Rockhampton.

WHEN: December migration

WHAT TO LOOK OUT FOR: Water pythons are a dark olive and pale yellow. They grow up to three metres and live up to 20 years. They are not poisonous but can give you a strong and painful bite.

© Greg Brown

Every summer, water pythons follow behind a stampede of rats heading for the hills.

other things to look out for

January

* Native grasses set seed
* Birds feed chicks
* Grasstrees flowering
* Snakes lay eggs
* Christmas bells flower in swamps
* Blowflies buzzing and breeding

February

* Eels go down rivers to sea
* Mullets run up east coast rivers
* Mistletoe birds breeding
* Marine snails leave tracks on beach
* Robber flies catch insect prey

March

* Brush-tail and Ringtail Possums give birth
* Goannas shed skin
* Seahorses lay eggs
* Blackberries ripe to pick
* Fruit bats mate
* Gymea Lily forms massive flower

April

* Fungi begin to push up
* Rainbow bee-eaters migrate north
* Greenhood orchids start to appear
* Mutton birds migrating
* Swamp mahogany flowers

May

* Meteor showers common
* Caterpillars into leaves
* Noisy Miners defend territory
* Dingoes mating
* Abundant rainfall in southern Australia
* Wombats breeding

June

* Visits from Antarctic birds
* Plovers lay eggs on ground
* White-breasted Sea Eagle nests
* Puffball fungi push up through the road
* Wedgetail Eagles pair up

Other things to look out for

July

* Young galahs fly about in flocks
* Some flatheads spawning (east coast)
* Masked Plovers nest
* Satin Bowerbirds decorate bower
* Spotted gum in flower

August

* Birds begin nesting
* Eastern rosellas pair up
* Bandicoots breeding
* Sawfly grubs devour gum leaves
* Young foxes explore
* Pardalotes dig nest burrows

September

* White cypress shed pollen
* Patterson's curse (Salvation Jane) flowering
* Channel-billed cuckoos arrive
* Antichinus babies born
* Millipedes enter homes

October

* Freshwater catfish build stone nests (east coast rivers)
* Flannel flowers appear
* Crabs mating
* Carnivorous plants flower
* Dead Muttonbirds on beaches

November

* Dollar birds look for nests (Qld)
* Lacewings emerge
* Frillneck lizards mate
* Paperbarks start flowering

December

* Terns nesting on reefs and beaches
* Bluebottles wash up on beaches
* River Redgums shed bark
* Jabirus lay eggs
* Newly hatched turtles head to sea

The history of Scribbly Gum

The Scribbly Gum website is part of The Lab, the ABC's science gateway. The stories were originally based on episodes of Green and Practical, a weekly environmental radio show broadcast on ABC Radio National. Audio clips from the show were put up on the web, along with text and images, making it one of the earliest interactive multimedia ABC websites. Later features were written specifically for Scribbly Gum, with many images supplied by researchers whose works were featured in the stories.

Along with the stories, a popular nature forum was launched and still runs today. The forum discusses topics such as how to trap Indian Myna birds, how to care for injured lizards and how to identify fungi.

The idea behind Scribbly Gum is that nature goes through yearly cycles, with each month bringing new and exciting changes in the bush, on the beaches and in the ocean. To see some of these events require travelling long distances or going to obscure places, but other changes, such as birds migrating and seasonal weather patterns, can be seen just by looking out the window.

Today, the Scribbly Gum website and forum attracts an enthusiastic and loyal audience from all over Australia. Visit the website at:

www.abc.net.au/science/scribblygum

About the author

Abbie Thomas is a science writer and producer with the ABC and holds an honours degree in Science (majoring in fish parasitology) from Macquarie University. She confesses to a long-term love affair with the Australian bush. As a 10 year old exploring the forests for animals and plants, she decided that she wanted to host a nature television show one day. After 15 years as a science and environment reporter, she has interviewed hundreds of researchers and experienced some pretty wild places in search of stories, including visiting a seal colony on an extinct volcanic island; climbing to the top of a 40-metre gum tree; dodging hippos while rafting the Zambezi River; and hunting coconut crabs in Vanuatu. Her most memorable job though, was work experience at the Australian Museum where she was given the delightful task of cleaning out the spider bottles. Abbie is married to palaeontologist and ABC science reporter Dr Paul Willis. She's still waiting for that TV show offer.

Index

Index

Acknowledgments

Many thanks to all those inspiring Australian scientists who so generously gave their time and expertise in the researching of the Scribbly Gum website and this book. Thanks in particular to Ted Edwards, Roger Sullivan, Barbara Triggs, Teresa Lebel, the Gould League (Vic), Birds Australia, Bob Beale, Richard Morecroft, Steve Parish, Ian Allen, Kylie Andrews, Janet Parker, Rachel Sullivan, Lynne Malcolm, Amanda Armstrong and Peter Jacklin. Thanks also to editor Sandra Davies and graphic designer Melanie Young, for their perfectionism and inspiration.

Many thanks to the following people who have contributed their photos: Neil Saunders, Peter Gill, Brett Crich, Keith Power, Greer Versteeg, Jason Dare, Alf Adams, Phillip Island Nature Parks, Lui Weber, Skot Biner, Paul Willis, Euan Ritchie, Fiona Hogan, David Nelson, Suzanne Gibson, Dean Nicolle, Linda Broome, Peter Chew, Charles Bulwinkel, David Hunter, Barbara Smith, Matt Herring, Stephen Lin, Sue Lewty, Teresa Lebel, Peter Collins, Russell White, Charm Venn, Michael Smith, Jess Daly, Matthew Sullivan, Alan Kwok, David Priddel, Dick Marks (Australian Koala Foundation), Lyn Lowe, Mark Norman, Michael Bath, Mark Hinder, Angus Hawke and Greg Brown.